I0162716

Haruna's Story Part 2

I Talk You Talk Press

CONTENTS

IMPORTANT!

This book is Part 2 of Haruna's Story. The story starts in *Haruna's Story Part 1*.

In this story, there are some Japanese words.
The Japanese words are
1. *shacho* - Company President/CEO
2. *san* - Mr/Ms (E.g. Tanaka san = Mr Tanaka)
3. *Izumo* - a city in Japan
4. *Matsue* - a city in Japan
5. *guzen* - a coincidence

CHAPTER ONE

Haruna is at Narita Airport. She will get on the airplane in two hours. She is going to LA to work in the Nice Ume-leaf Cosmetics LA shop. She goes into a duty-free shop in the airport and looks at the cosmetics. There are many famous brands. There is also a Nice Ume-leaf Cosmetics counter.

"Hi," says Haruna to Mie Yamamoto, the Nice Ume-leaf Cosmetics counter saleswoman.

"Oh, hi Yamane san!" says Mie. "How are you?"

"I'm fine thanks, but I feel a little nervous. I hope I can do a good job in LA," says Haruna.

"You will do a good job, Yamane san. You are a very good worker," says Mie.

"Thank you Yamamoto san. But I'm worried about my English," says Haruna.

"Don't worry! You got a high TOEIC score! Your English is very good!" says Mie. "Oh! Look! There's Matsumoto san at the Chanel counter!"

Haruna looks at the Chanel counter. Kana is looking at mascara.

"Matsumoto san, hi!" says Mie.

"Oh, hi Yamamoto san!" says Kana. She looks at Haruna.

"Good morning, Yamane san."

"Good morning, Matsumoto san," says Haruna.

"What are you talking about?" asks Kana.

"We are talking about English," says Mie. "Yamane san is nervous. She is worried about her English. Are you worried Matsumoto san?"

"No, of course not!" says Kana. "I have been to New York many times."

"Really?" asks Mie.

"Yes. And I have many American friends in New York," says Kana.

"Well, good luck in New York, Matsumoto san," says Haruna. "I have to go now. I need to buy some water."

"Good luck in LA, Yamane san," says Kana. "Let's work hard and enjoy our time in the USA."

"Yes, let's do that," says Haruna. She does not want to talk to Kana.

At last the airplane takes off. Haruna looks out of the window. She can see all of Tokyo and the mountains below. She feels a little sad. She is leaving her friends and family for a year. She will miss everyone, and she will miss Japan. Then, the airplane goes up into the clouds and she cannot see anything. She closes her eyes, and very soon, she falls asleep.

CHAPTER TWO

Haruna arrives at LA airport. She gets off the airplane and walks to Immigration. She has to wait for a long time. She slept a little on the airplane, but she feels tired. She wants to get to her apartment quickly. She wants to relax before her job starts.

"Next!" The immigration officer shouts to Haruna.

She smiles and walks up to the counter. The immigration officer does not smile.

"Can I see your passport?" says the immigration officer.

"Yes, here you are," says Haruna. She gives him her passport. He looks at her passport very carefully.

"What is the purpose of your visit to the USA?" says the immigration officer.

"Pardon? I don't understand," says Haruna. The immigration officer is speaking very fast. She cannot catch his words.

"The purpose of your visit! The purpose! Why did you come to the USA? Sightseeing? Business? Study? The purpose!" he says.

"Oh, business," says Haruna.

"Show me your working visa!" says the immigration officer.

"Here you are." Haruna shows him her visa.

"How long are you going to stay in the USA?" asks the officer.

"I'm going to stay for a year," says Haruna.

The officer stamps her passport. "Okay. Here you are." He gives Haruna her passport.

"Thank you very much," says Haruna.

She walks to the baggage area and waits for her suitcase. There are many people waiting. After ten minutes, she sees her suitcase.

Haruna takes her suitcase and walks out of the airport. It is very hot and sunny, and there are many people. She feels very tired. She gets into a taxi.

"Where to?" asks the taxi driver.

Haruna gives the driver a map to her new apartment. "Here please," she says.

Haruna looks out of the taxi window. The roads are very wide. There are many big cars. It looks very different from Japan. *I'm in LA! I'm in America!* she thinks. She feels excited.

It takes around thirty minutes to get from the airport to her apartment. The taxi arrives at her apartment. She looks in her bag for her purse.

Where is my purse? thinks Haruna. She cannot find her purse. She starts to panic. She takes everything out of her bag. *Passport, lipstick, tissues, pen, notebook…ah! My purse! Here it is!* Haruna finds her purse. She pays the driver and gives him a $5 tip.

Nice Ume-leaf Cosmetics has rented an apartment in LA for Haruna. She will stay in this apartment for a year. The apartment is number 202. She goes to number 202 and opens her bag. She looks for her key. Her key is not in her bag. Haruna starts to panic. "Where is my key? Oh no! I can't find my key! Where is it?" she says.

Haruna's key dropped out of her bag in the taxi. She does not know what to do. She does not know anybody in LA. She sits down outside the apartment in the hot sunshine. This is not a good start to her new life in LA. She has no key, so she cannot get into her apartment. Haruna closes her eyes. The sun is very hot. She feels very sleepy. She sits there for about an hour. She is too tired to move.

"Are you OK?"

Haruna looks up. A young man is standing next to her. He has dark brown hair and brown eyes. He is smiling.

"What's wrong?" asks the man.

Haruna stands up. "I can't find my apartment key," says Haruna. "I dropped it in the taxi."

"Is this your apartment?" asks the man.

"Yes, number 202 is my apartment," says Haruna.

"It's OK. The apartment block manager has a key. She can help you. Where are you from?" asks the man.

"I'm from Japan," says Haruna.

"From Japan? My brother lives in Japan," says the man.

"Oh really? Where does he live?" asks Haruna.

"He lives in a beautiful place. Do you know Izumo?" asks the man.

"Izumo? Yes! Izumo is near my hometown!" says Haruna. She is very surprised.

"Oh really? Where is your hometown?" asks the man.

"My hometown is Matsue," says Haruna.

"Oh yes! Matsue!" The man takes his smartphone out of his pocket. "I know Matsue. My brother sent me a photograph of Matsue."

The man shows Haruna the photograph on his smartphone.

"Matsue-jo!" says Haruna.

"Yes, Matsue Castle! It is very beautiful. I want to visit it someday," says the man.

"*Guzen!*" says Haruna.

"Pardon? What is *guzen?*" asks the man.

Haruna cannot remember the English word for *guzen*.

"Well, I'm from Matsue, and you have a photograph of Matsue castle. That is *guzen*," she says.

"Do you mean it is 'a coincidence'?" asks the man. "Is *guzen* Japanese for coincidence?"

"Coincidence? Yes! That's it! It's a coincidence!" says Haruna. Now she remembers the word.

"I'm David," says the man. He holds his right hand out. "Nice to meet you."

"I'm Haruna. Nice to meet you, too," says Haruna. She shakes hands with David.

"Let's go and find the apartment manager," says David.

They walk down to the ground floor. There is a small office. A woman is sitting behind the desk. She is the apartment block manager. She looks up at David and Haruna and smiles.

David explains the situation to the manager. She listens very carefully. Haruna shows the manager her passport, and then, the manager gives Haruna a spare key.

Haruna and David walk out of the office and into the afternoon sunshine. Haruna suddenly feels very tired.

"Thank you David! Thank you so much!" says Haruna.

"You're welcome. I have to go to work now," says David. "I hope we can meet again. I would like to talk to you about Matsue and

Izumo. And if you need any help in LA, please ask me. I am your neighbour. I live in apartment number 204."

"Thank you! I hope we can meet again, too. Bye!" says Haruna. David waves goodbye and gets into a car in the car park.

That was lucky! thinks Haruna.

Haruna opens the door of her apartment and walks inside. It is a big apartment. It is much bigger than her apartment in Tokyo. There is living room with a TV and a sofa. In the bedroom there is a bed and a large closet. The kitchen dining area is big. There is an oven, a sink, a microwave oven, a toaster and a kettle in the kitchen. The window in the living room is very large. She opens the window and looks out. Next to the apartment is a big supermarket. There are many people and many cars.

Wow! This is LA! thinks Haruna. She closes the curtains and sits down on the sofa. She feels very sleepy. She falls asleep.

CHAPTER THREE

Haruna wakes up at 7:00am. It is Saturday. Her mobile phone is ringing. She answers the phone. "Hello?"

"Yamane san, this is Takahashi."

"Takahashi shacho! Good morning!" says Haruna.

Haruna is very surprised. *Why is Takahashi shacho calling at this time?*

"The shop in LA will open on Monday at 9:00am. At 8:00am today, the boxes of cosmetics will arrive at the shop. There are five boxes of cosmetics and five boxes of skincare products. Put the cosmetics on the counters near the shop window, and put the skincare products on the display at the back of the shop. There is also a box of posters and pamphlets. Put the posters on the wall and put the pamphlets on the counter," says Takahashi shacho.

"Yes, Takahashi shacho," says Haruna.

"Your shop has two American workers. Their names are Emma and Angela. Emma is a skincare expert. She worked for a famous company for many years. Angela is a cosmetics expert. She is a very good saleswoman. They will start working on Monday morning."

"I understand," says Haruna.

"If you have any problems, call me or email me," says Takahashi shacho.

"Yes, Takahashi shacho," says Haruna.

"I spoke to Matsumoto san in New York. When she arrived in New York, she didn't go to her apartment. She didn't sleep. She took a taxi from the airport to the shop. She started working," says Takahashi shacho. "What did you do?"

"I came to my apartment and I slept," says Haruna. She is very shocked. Kana always works so hard!

"Yamane san, you have to work hard in America. I want Nice Ume-leaf Cosmetics to be a famous and popular brand in the USA. Do you understand?" says Takahashi shacho.

"Yes, I understand. I will work hard," says Haruna. She finishes the phone call. She is still very tired, but she must go to work.

CHAPTER FOUR

It is nine o' clock on Saturday night. Haruna is in the shop. She is very tired. In the morning, she cleaned the shop. In the afternoon, she put the cosmetics on the counter. She put the skincare products on the display at the back of the shop. In the evening, she put the posters on the walls and she put the pamphlets on the counter. She has worked very hard. The shop looks very nice. Haruna understands shop design very well.

At the back of the shop is a small staff room. In the staff room, there is a table and some chairs. There is also a kettle and some cups. She goes to the staff room to make a cup of coffee. She sits down at the table. Then, the shop telephone rings.

Who is calling me? she wonders. She goes back into the shop and answers the phone.

"Hello, Nice Ume-leaf Cosmetics, LA shop, Haruna Yamane speaking," says Haruna.

"It's Matsumoto."

"Matsumoto san!" says Haruna. "What time is it in New York now?"

"It is very late. But I'm still working at the shop. How is LA?" asks Kana.

"It is very hot, and there are many people," says Haruna. "How is New York?"

"New York is great," says Kana. "The Nice Ume-leaf Cosmetics New York shop is very nice. It is very big. It is near 5th Avenue. Is the LA shop big?" asks Kana.

"No, it isn't so big," says Haruna. "It's a small boutique. But it's on a very busy road. There are many boutiques here, and there is a large department store near the shop. But I am nervous. I hope many people come to the shop on Monday."

"Tell me about your opening event," says Kana.

"Opening event? I don't have an opening event," says Haruna.

"Really? You don't have an opening event?" Kana is surprised. "I am planning a big opening event on Sunday night in New York."

Haruna is surprised.

"What kind of opening event?" asks Haruna.

"My opening event is a wine party. I sent a press release to all the newspapers and TV stations in New York. Many newspaper reporters, photographers and two TV cameramen will come to my opening event," says Kana.

Haruna is shocked. She didn't think about an opening event.

"And, my friend in New York has a sister. Her sister is a famous model. She will come to the opening event too. So, I think the New York shop will be very busy and famous," says Kana. "Good luck Yamane san! Goodbye!"

"Goodbye Matsumoto san," says Haruna.

Haruna has no opening event. She did not think about an opening event. No newspaper reporters or cameramen will come to her shop on Monday.

Why didn't I plan an opening event? Why didn't Matsumoto san tell me about her idea? I have to work harder! I have to plan many events and campaigns! thinks Haruna.

Haruna switches the lights off and locks the shop door. She walks home. On the way home, she stops at the supermarket and buys some chocolate. She always eats chocolate when she feels tired.

She goes back to her apartment. She makes a cup of tea and eats the chocolate. It is delicious. She sits on the sofa in the living room. She switches on her computer. There is an email from Julie.

---Hi Haruna! How is LA? Are you having a good time? I miss you! I hope we can talk soon! On Monday, my family and friends will go to your shop. They want to meet you and they want to buy Nice Ume-leaf Cosmetics! Good luck! From Julie---

Haruna writes a reply.

---Hi Julie! Thank you for your email. LA is very hot. Today I worked in the shop from morning to night. I am very tired. I am very worried about Monday.

I hope many customers will come to the shop. I am looking forward to seeing your family and friends. I will write again soon. From Haruna---

Haruna goes to bed, but she can't sleep. She is worried about Monday. How many customers will come to the shop?

CHAPTER FIVE

It is 7:30am on Monday morning. Haruna is in the shop. She got up at 5:00am. She could not sleep on Sunday night because she was excited about the opening day. She looks around the shop. The layout is perfect.

The door opens. Two American women walk into the shop.

"Good morning! Are you Haruna Yamane, the shop manager?" says one of the women. She has short black hair, and her make-up is very natural.

"Yes, I am," says Haruna.

"I'm Emma. Nice to meet you," says the woman.

"Hello Emma. Nice to meet you, too!"

Haruna smiles and shakes hands with Emma.

"I'm Angela. Nice to meet you," says the other woman. She has long red hair and a big smile. She is wearing a lot of make-up.

"Nice to meet you Angela," says Haruna.

She shakes hands with Angela.

"We are very excited to work for Nice Ume-leaf Cosmetics," says Emma.

"I hope American women like our products," says Haruna.

"I think all American women will like Nice Ume-leaf Cosmetics," says Angela. "Nice Ume-leaf Cosmetics are very good quality."

Emma and Angela are very friendly. They have a meeting for an hour. Haruna tells Emma and Angela about the products. She also tells them about the sales targets. Haruna has made many sales plans. She wants Emma and Angela to sell many products. In the meeting,

Emma and Angela listen carefully to Haruna. She has many ideas. Emma and Angela like Haruna. They think she will be a good leader and a hard worker.

It is 9:00am.

Haruna opens the shop door.

"We are open!" says Angela. "Congratulations!"

"Congratulations!" says Emma.

"Thank you! Let's do our best!" says Haruna.

"Yes, let's do our best!" says Angela.

At 9:10, two customers come into the shop. They look at the cosmetics.

"Can I help you?" asks Emma.

"No, thank you. We are just looking," says one of the women.

They look at the skincare products. Then, they leave the shop. They don't buy any products.

"Emma, 'can I help you?' is not a good question to ask," says Haruna. "Many people will say 'no'. I think we should show the customers some cosmetics, and give them some samples."

"Yes, that's a good idea," says Emma.

Another customer comes into the shop. Emma shows her some cosmetics, and she gives the customer some samples. The customer takes the samples, but she doesn't buy any products.

Haruna starts to worry a little.

Then at 10:00, two well-dressed women come to the shop.

"Nice Ume-leaf Cosmetics! We love Nice Ume-leaf Cosmetics!" says one of the women. "My friend Julie sends me Nice Ume-leaf Cosmetics from Japan. Are you Haruna?"

"Yes, I am. I am Julie's friend," says Haruna.

"Haruna, I'd like to buy a lipstick. Which colour is best for me?" says the woman.

Haruna chooses a pink lipstick for the woman. "How about this?" asks Haruna.

She puts the lipstick on the woman's lips. The woman looks in the mirror.

"Yes, it is very nice. I'll take it. And, I want a nice eye shadow too."

Emma and Angela help the other woman. The women buy a few products.

"Thanks Haruna! We will come back again soon!" say the women.

"Congratulations Haruna! That is our first sale!" says Angela.

Haruna smiles. She is feeling more confident now.

In the afternoon, a few more customers come to the shop. Haruna gives all the customers some free samples. Many customers are interested in Nice Ume-leaf Cosmetics. They ask many questions. Emma and Angela put cosmetics on some customers. Some stay in the shop for a long time, and some buy many cosmetics.

The cosmetics are high quality, so they are expensive. Haruna watches the customers. Many customers look very rich. They have brand name bags, like Chanel and Louis Vuitton, and all of them are very well-dressed.

It is 7:00pm. The first day has finished!

Haruna closes the front door of the shop and goes to the cash register. Most customers paid by credit card, so she counts the credit card receipts.

The total sales amount for the first day is $3000. It is very low. The daily sales target is $10,000.

She goes to the staff room and switches the kettle on. She needs a cup of coffee. Then, the phone rings.

"Hello, Nice Ume-leaf Cosmetics, LA shop, Haruna Yamane speaking," says Haruna.

"It's Takahashi," says Takahashi shacho.

"Hello, Takahashi shacho," says Haruna.

"How was the first day?" asks Takahashi shacho.

"We had many customers, but they did not buy many products," says Haruna.

"How much money did you take?"

"We took $3000," says Haruna.

"Only $3000? Why didn't the customers buy more products?" asks Takahashi shacho.

"I don't know. Maybe it is because Nice Ume-leaf Cosmetics is a new shop in LA. Many people here don't know about Nice Ume-leaf Cosmetics," says Haruna.

"Yamane san, Nice Ume-leaf Cosmetics is a new shop in New York, too. But the New York shop took $20,000," says Takahashi shacho.

"$20,000! Really?" Haruna is shocked.

"Yes! $20,000. Matsumoto san had a wine party opening event on

Sunday night. Many newspaper reporters and TV cameramen went to the wine party. A famous model also went to the party. She bought many Nice Ume-leaf Cosmetics goods," says Takahashi shacho.

"What opening event did you have, Yamane san?"

"I didn't have an event, Takahashi shacho. I'm sorry," says Haruna.

"Yamane san, you have to work harder! Your sales target for this week is $70,000!" says Takahashi shacho.

"Yes, Takahashi shacho. I understand," Haruna says. She must try harder!

CHAPTER SIX

It is October.

Haruna has been in LA for six months. She is working very hard. She starts work at 8:00am and finishes at 10:00pm every day. She has many good ideas. She started an English Facebook page for Nice Ume-leaf Cosmetics LA shop. She started an English blog about cosmetics and beauty. Emma and Angela help to write blog posts about skincare. Haruna also changed the shop layout. Takahashi shacho calls her every day. He is never happy. The monthly target is $280,000. Last month, Haruna's shop only took $140,000. The New York shop took $300,000. Haruna is trying her best, but Kana always sells more.

It is 8:00am on Thursday morning. Haruna is leaving her apartment.

"Good morning, Haruna!" says David.

"Oh, hi David! Long time no see! How are you?" says Haruna. She hasn't seen David for a few months.

"I'm fine thank you. Are you going to work now?" says David.

"Yes, I am. Are you going to work?" says Haruna.

"Yes, I am."

"What do you do?" asks Haruna.

"I work in a movie studio near the Grand Department Store. I'm a cameraman," says David.

"Really? Wow! That's exciting!" says Haruna. She is very surprised. David works in a movie studio!

"It's not exciting. In LA, many people work in studios," says

David. "It's a normal job."

"Do you meet many famous people?" asks Haruna.

"Yes, I do. But, famous people are people. Like you and me. We are all the same. They are not special," says David. "Where do you work, Haruna?"

"I work in a cosmetics shop near the department store," says Haruna.

"Oh really? How do you get there?"

"I walk," says Haruna.

"You walk? It's too hot to walk!" says David. "I drive to work. Would you like to come with me in my car?"

"Yes, thank you. You are very kind," says Haruna.

Haruna sits in David's car. It is very big.

"So, how is your job at the cosmetics company?" asks David.

"I enjoy it very much. I like cosmetics, I like my staff and I like my customers here in LA," says Haruna. "But, I have to sell more cosmetics. Every day, my boss calls me and he is very angry."

"Oh, that's too bad," says David. "What is your shop's name?"

"It is Nice Ume-leaf Cosmetics," says Haruna.

"Nice Ume-leaf Cosmetics? I don't know it," says David.

"It is a Japanese company. It is very famous in Japan," says Haruna.

"Oh really? I think Japanese products are very high quality. I think American women will like your cosmetics very much," says David.

"Thank you," says Haruna. "I hope you are right."

Then, Haruna has an idea.

"David, do you have many female friends?" she asks.

"Yes, I do," says David. "I know a lot of women in the studio."

"Can you tell your female friends about Nice Ume-leaf Cosmetics?" asks Haruna.

She looks in her bag and takes out some pamphlets and some samples of foundation, powder and eye shadow.

"Here are some pamphlets about our cosmetics and some free samples. Could you give these pamphlets and free samples to your friends, please?" asks Haruna.

"Of course! I will give your pamphlets and samples to all my family and friends," says David.

"Thank you David," says Haruna.

Haruna likes David. He is very kind and handsome. She wants to ask him, "Do you have a girlfriend?" but she is too shy.

They arrive at Haruna's shop.

"Good luck today, Haruna. If you need any help, please ask me. I will try to help you," says David.

"Thank you very much David," says Haruna.

She gets out of the car and opens the shop.

It is 5:00pm. Haruna is very tired. She goes to the staff room to make a cup of coffee. She hears a customer come into the shop.

"Good evening sir," says Angela.

"Good evening," says the customer.

Haruna is surprised. The customer is a man.

"How can I help you?" asks Angela.

"I'd like to buy some cosmetics," says the man.

I know that voice! Who is it? Ah yes! It's David! thinks Haruna. *David is here! He's buying cosmetics. But…why is he buying cosmetics?*

"Are the cosmetics for your girlfriend or your wife?" asks Angela.

"They are a present for my girlfriend," says David.

Haruna is shocked. *Oh no! David has a girlfriend!*

Angela chooses some cosmetics for David. She puts the cosmetics in a beautiful box.

"Here you are. That's 250 dollars please," says Angela.

David gives Angela the money.

"Thank you very much. Have a nice evening!" says Angela.

"Thank you very much," says David. He leaves the shop.

Haruna walks to the counter.

"Angela, what did that man buy?" she asks.

"He bought some brown eye shadow, some mascara, a lipstick and some face cream," says Angela. "His girlfriend is very lucky! She has a nice boyfriend!"

"Yes, I think so too," says Haruna sadly.

CHAPTER SEVEN

(One week later.)

One morning, Haruna, Emma and Angela are working in the shop. A big man comes into the shop. He is wearing a black suit and big sunglasses.

"Can I speak to the manager?" he asks. He has a deep voice.

"Yes, I am the manager," says Haruna. "How can I help you?"

"I am Grace Lily's bodyguard," says the man.

"Grace Lily? The famous Hollywood actress?" says Haruna.

"Yes, that's right. Grace Lily wants to visit this shop this afternoon. She will come here at 1:00pm. She will visit with two bodyguards and an assistant. Also, there will be paparazzi," says the man.

"Paparazzi? What is 'paparazzi'?" asks Haruna.

"Paparazzi. Many photographers and newspaper reporters. They will take many pictures of Grace Lily and your shop," says the man. "See you later."

He leaves the shop.

Haruna, Angela and Emma are very excited.

"Grace Lily, the famous movie star, is coming to our shop! That's amazing!" says Emma.

"Oh wow! This is so cool!" says Angela.

"Why is a famous movie star coming to our shop?" asks Haruna.

"Haruna, this is LA. Many famous movie stars live here.

Sometimes, I see famous movie stars in the department store, or in restaurants. It's not so unusual," says Angela.

"I see," says Haruna.

Haruna is very excited, but very nervous. She has never met a famous person before!

Haruna looks at the clock. It is 1:00pm. She hears a noise outside the shop. She looks outside and sees a big, expensive car. Grace Lily, her bodyguards and assistant get out of the car and enter the shop. There are many photographers outside the shop. They are taking photographs of the shop and Grace Lily.

Grace is very slim and beautiful. She has very long brown hair, and she is wearing a long white dress. She is Hollywood's top actress. Her last movie was the top movie of the year. Many people say she will win many Oscars for the movie.

"Good afternoon, madam. Thank you for visiting our shop today," says Haruna. Her voice is shaking a little. *I hope my English pronunciation is okay!* She thinks.

"Good afternoon," says Grace. "I'd like to see some lipsticks, powder, and eye shadow."

"Yes, of course. Please take a seat at the counter. I will bring some cosmetics," says Haruna.

Grace sits down. Haruna brings a box of lipsticks, powder, and eye shadow. Haruna opens a lipstick.

"How about this colour, madam?" asks Haruna.

"Do you have pink? I like pink," says Grace.

"Yes, of course. How about this?" asks Haruna.

"Yes, I'll try it," says Grace.

Haruna puts the lipstick on Grace's lips. Grace looks in the mirror.

"It's very nice, thank you."

Next, Haruna shows Grace the eye shadow and puts it on Grace's eyes. Then, she puts the powder on Grace's face.

Grace looks in the mirror. "The quality of the cosmetics is very good," says Grace. "I like Japanese cosmetics."

"Thank you," says Haruna.

"What's your name?" asks Grace.

"My name is Haruna Yamane."

"Haruna, you are a very good make-up artist. I like your technique," says Grace.

"Thank you very much," says Haruna. She cannot believe it! She is talking to a movie star!

"Where did you study about cosmetics?" asks Grace.

"I studied in Japan. After university, I joined Nice Ume-leaf Cosmetics. In Nice Ume-leaf Cosmetics, I studied make up techniques for three years, then I became a cosmetics saleswoman," says Haruna.

"I am surprised. Your technique is very good. You are better than the movie studio makeup artist!" says Grace.

"Oh, thank you," says Haruna.

Grace buys many cosmetics.

"Thank you very much for coming today. Please come again," says Haruna.

"Thank you. Goodbye," says Grace.

Grace and her bodyguards and assistant leave the shop. The paparazzi follow Grace's car.

Haruna sits down. Angela brings her a cup of coffee.

"Good job Haruna!" says Emma. "Grace really liked you! And she likes our cosmetics!"

"Yes, great job Haruna!" says Angela.

"Was my English okay?" asks Haruna.

"Yes, your English was great!" says Angela. "Well done!"

Haruna feels so happy. A famous movie star likes her cosmetics and she likes her technique! Unbelievable!

"Emma, Angela, is this a dream?" asks Haruna.

Emma and Angela laugh. "A dream? No, of course not! It is real life! You are in LA now!" says Angela. "This is normal life!"

The next morning, Haruna buys some newspapers. There are many pictures of Grace Lily in the shop. There are also pictures of Haruna putting lipstick on Grace's lips. Haruna feels very happy and very proud. She carefully puts the newspaper in her bag. She will send it to her mother and father. They will be very surprised, and very happy.

Many people see the photographs in the newspaper and on the Internet and come to the shop. They want to buy make-up from Nice Ume-leaf Cosmetics.

Haruna's mobile phone rings.

"Hello?" says Haruna.

"Haruna, it's Julie! I read the LA and New York newspapers on the Internet. There are many photographs of you and Grace Lily! It's wonderful! Your shop is famous!" says Julie.

"Thank you, Julie," says Haruna.

"You sound tired Haruna. How is LA? Do you have any new friends?" asks Julie.

"Well, I work very hard every day, so I don't have time to make any new friends," says Haruna. "But, in my apartment block, there is a nice man. His name is David."

"Really? Do you like him?" asks Julie.

"Yes, I do. He is very kind. But I think he has a girlfriend," says Haruna.

"Oh, that's too bad," says Julie.

"Yes. But I have to focus on my job, so I have no time for dating," says Haruna.

"Yes, I think your shop will be very busy. It is very famous now," says Julie. "And there are many other men in Los Angeles!"

CHAPTER EIGHT

Every day, many customers come to Haruna's shop. Many customers also go to the shop in New York.

At the end of the month, Haruna checks the sales figures.

LA shop: $350,000. New York shop: $310,000.

"Emma! Angela! Look! Our sales are higher than the New York shop!" says Haruna.

Emma and Angela look at the computer.

"That's great Haruna! Let's celebrate!" says Emma.

"Celebrate?" asks Haruna.

"Yes! Let's go for dinner. Haruna, you work hard every day. You need to rest a little and enjoy LA. Let's go to the Italian restaurant in the next street," says Angela.

That evening, Haruna, Emma and Angela go to the Italian restaurant. They eat delicious pasta and pizza and drink lots of red wine. They talk about many things. Emma and Angela are very interested in Japan. They ask Haruna many questions. Haruna asks Emma and Angela many questions about their lives. They have a very good time.

"How about dessert?" asks Angela. "The ice-cream here is amazing. You have to try it Haruna."

"Sure! Sounds good!" says Haruna.

Then, Haruna's mobile phone rings.

"Hello?" says Haruna.

"It's Takahashi."

"Hello Takahashi shacho," says Haruna.

"Yamane san, you did a very good job this month. Well done," says Takahashi shacho.

"Thank you Takahashi shacho," says Haruna. She is very happy. Takahashi shacho rarely says good things.

"Yamane san, Grace Lily's assistant called our office in Tokyo today," says Takahashi shacho.

"Really?"

"Yes. Tomorrow, Grace Lily will come to your shop. She wants to talk to you," says Takahashi shacho.

"She wants to talk to me?" asks Haruna. She is very surprised. "Why?"

"She wants to ask you something very important."

"About cosmetics?" asks Haruna.

"About a movie," says Takahashi shacho.

"A movie? I don't understand," says Haruna.

"Grace Lily will tell you tomorrow," says Takahashi shacho. "Yamane san, you must say 'yes'."

"OK, I will. I will say 'yes'. Goodbye," says Haruna.

"Are you okay Haruna?" asks Emma.

"That was strange," says Haruna. "Grace Lily wants to talk to me tomorrow. I wonder why?"

"Yeah, that's strange. But our ice-cream is here! You can find out tomorrow. Now, let's eat!"

Haruna starts to eat the ice-cream. It is very delicious, but she cannot stop thinking about tomorrow. *What will happen tomorrow?*

Find out in Haruna's Story Part 3.

THANK YOU

Thank you for reading Haruna's Story Part 2! We hope you enjoyed the story. (Word count: 5,690)

There are quizzes about this book on our free study site I Talk You Talk Press EXTRA. http://italk-youtalk.com

If you would like to read more graded readers, please visit our website
http://www.italkyoutalk.com

Other Level 1 graded readers include
A Business Trip to New York
A Homestay in Auckland
A Trip to London
Dear Ellen
Haruna's Story Part 1
Haruna's Story Part 3
Ken's Story Part 1
Ken's Story Part 2
Life is Surprising!
Strange Stories
The Christmas Present
The Old Hospital
We Met Online

ABOUT THE AUTHOR

I Talk You Talk Press is a Japan-based publisher of language textbooks, graded readers and language learning/teaching resources.

Our team is made up of highly experienced language teachers and translators, who have all studied at least one additional language to an advanced level.

This experience enables us to design our materials from the perspective of both the teacher and the learner. We consult with both teachers and language learners when designing our textbooks and graded readers, and test our materials extensively in the classroom before publication.

We are a fast-growing press, and currently publish graded readers for learners of English. We publish new graded readers monthly.